"*PageLand* will challenge you to think about your life from beginning to end and what really matters."
— Bo Boshers, Executive Director, Willow Creek Association Student Ministries

"As a lover of books, I think *PageLand* is brilliantly fun—a refreshing new way to tell a wonderful old story."
— Melody Carlson, Author, *Angels in the Snow, Looking for Cassandra Jane, Blood Sisters,* and "Diary of a Teenage Girl" Series

"Truth is stranger than fantasy, but in the fantasy of *PageLand,* expect to encounter truth."
— Gary D. Chapman, Ph.D., Author, *The Five Love Languages*

"The ideal book for the overeducated atheist."
— John Cherry, Director and Creator, the *Earnest* Films

"What a fresh and creative presentation of a timeless and essential message—and perhaps what is most brilliant is that there is something in *PageLand* for every age."
— David Durham, Director, The Crucible, Nashville, Tennessee

"David Hutchens has written a book that is unsettling—for children certainly, not for me—and yet I had to finish it and close the pages to make sure I was still alive. I am, you know."
— Jack Hafer, Film Producer

"If you want to reflect on the mysteries of creation, the fall, and redemption, you could read the great theologians: Augustine, Aquinas, Barth, Kant, Moltmann, Tillich, and the rest . . . or, you could read *PageLand.* If you wanted to gain a vivid overview of time, eternity, and the destiny of the human soul, you could read Thomas à Kempis, C. S. Lewis, Thomas Merton . . . or, you could read *PageLand.*

"All kidding aside, David Hutchens and Bobby Gombert have crafted a retelling of the Grand Story that is truly incarnational, on several levels. Until you read *PageLand*, you won't believe it's possible to pack so many immense ideas into so few pages.

"C. S. Lewis said, 'If you can't express your faith in the vernacular, either you don't understand it, or you don't really believe it.' Hutchens and Gombert clearly understand and truly believe. Want to know how I can tell? . . . Just read *PageLand*."

— Thom Lemmons, Author, the "Daughters of Faith" Series and *Jabez: A Novel*

"*PageLand:* a simple, charming little story that becomes the gospel in allegory form."

— Ray and Anne Ortlund, Renewal Ministries, Newport Beach, California

"In the pages of this remarkable little book, you will enter a world that exists here and nowhere else. And yet the story it tells is a story you've heard before, only you've never heard it like this. *PageLand* is all about love and sharing and some funny little creatures who teach us the Good News all over again. Buy two copies of this book—one to keep (you'll want to read it more than once because it makes you smile) and one to give to a friend who needs to know the truth but doesn't want to read anything religious.

"I promise you: this book flies 'under the radar' and right into the heart. I've never read anything like it. It stands as a delightful story, well told, wonderfully illustrated, and (in case you missed it before) it makes you smile. How many books make you do that? I hope that David Hutchens and Bobby Gombert will take us back to *PageLand* in the future. I'd like to know what happens next."

— Dr. Ray Pritchard, Senior Pastor, Calvary Memorial Church, Oak Park, Illinois
    Author, *He's God and We're Not, And When You Pray, In the Shadow of the Cross,*
    and *FAQ*

"What an absolutely delightful book! Anyone who walks through its pages will gasp at the elegant simplicity. Anyone who takes its message to heart will discover new possibilities for relationships—and life!"
— Rubel Shelly, Preaching Minister,
Family of God at Woodmont Hills, Nashville, Tennessee

"With a hint of Lewis and Tolkein between the lines, Hutchens brings to bear through delightful story (and the quirky illustrations by Bob Gombert) the tensions involved in living a lifestyle of love, and sharing and working together."
— Rev. Byron Spradlin, President,
Artists in Christian Testimony

"*PageLand* is a page-*turner*. This is the kind of book I will give to friends and even strangers in the airport. I was bound in PageLand and then set free."
— Greg Taylor, Author, *High Places*, Editor of *NEW Wineskins* Magazine

"David Hutchens and Bobby Gombert have taken the timeless truth of the gospel and dressed it in new clothes. The turn of phrase is relevant and contemporary, and the art is engaging and charming. This team uses their gifts to engage readers of all ages with the eternally hopeful news of God's redemptive plan for his creation."
— Kim Thomas, Painter, Author, Recording Artist

"*PageLand* is a wonder. It's hard to believe that such a small volume could both delight children with a fresh, clever, and engaging story *and* enthrall adults with its stunning insight into the relationship between God and humankind."
— Thomas Williams, Novelist,
Coauthor with Josh McDowell, *In Search of Certainty*

PageLand

A Story about Love and Sharing and Working Together

by David Hutchens
illustrated by Bobby Gombert

0-8054-2726-0

Published by Broadman & Holman Publishers, Nashville, Tennessee

Dewey Decimal Classification: F
Subject Heading: BIBLE. N. T. GOSPELS—FICTION \ GOSPEL—FICTION

Scripture citation is from the Holy Bible, New International Version, © 1973, 1978, 1984 by
International Bible Society.

Hi. Welcome to this book.
It's called *PageLand*.

This is a story about
love and sharing and working together.

To Landon

"Happy Hallowen"/05

Love Liz

See those little creatures below? They are the *characters*. That means they live only within the pages of this book.

Since you are the reader of this book, the characters can't see you or hear you. They can't smell you either. So if you have bad breath, there's no need to be concerned.

In fact, the characters don't even know they live in a book called *PageLand*. They just go from one page to the next without thinking about it — just as we live from one day to the next without thinking about it.

That's OK, because *PageLand* is a nice place to live. It is, after all, a story about love and sharing and working together.

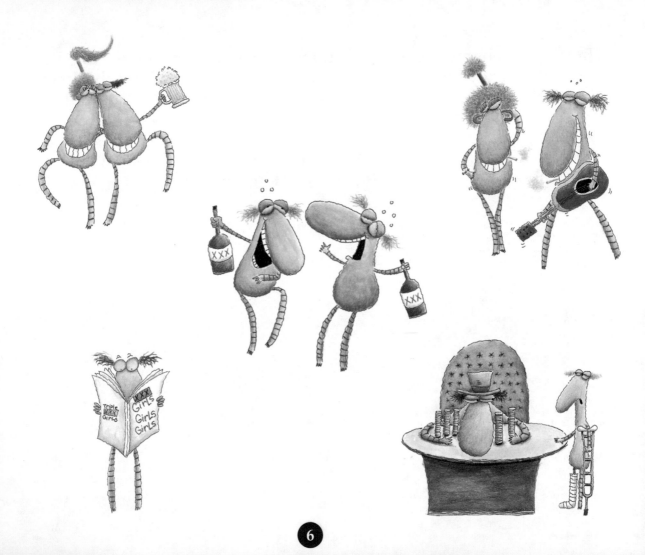

6

OK. Maybe not.

7

There seems to be a problem with your copy
of *PageLand*. The characters have gone
berserk.

Look at them — making a mess of
the pages. Playing out in the mar-
gins. Sleeping in the gutter
where the pages come together.

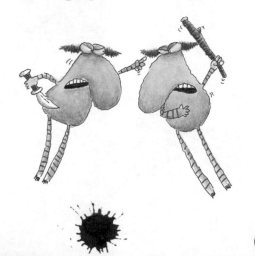

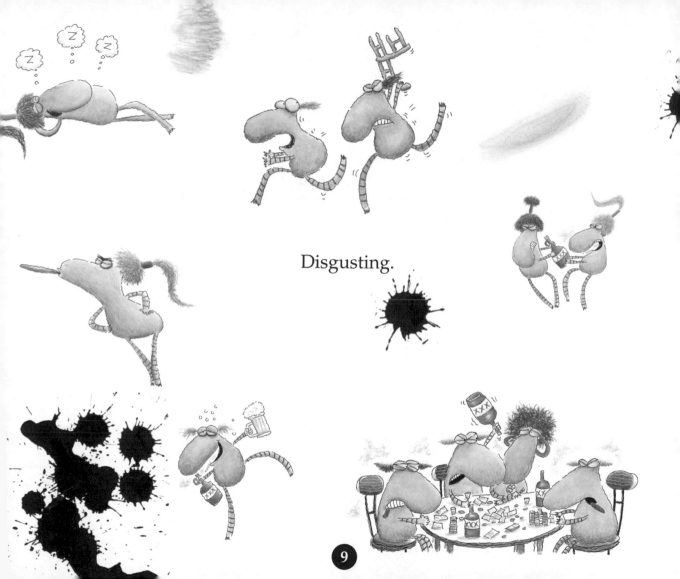

Disgusting.

9

The author, who created *PageLand*
and wrote these words that
you are reading right now, was not pleased.

So one day, a giant loud speaker suddenly appeared in the middle of the page, out of nowhere.

(Yes, this is a pretty strange thing to happen. But remember, the author created *PageLand*, and he can make anything happen he wants.)

"People!" came a voice booming from the speaker. Everybody stopped and looked up, amazed and frightened.

The voice continued. "This is the author speaking. I'm not happy with the way you are acting in my book. I want this to be a happy story about love and sharing and working together. OK?"

A murmur went up in the crowd.

"How did that loud speaker just appear up in the middle of the air like that?" someone said.

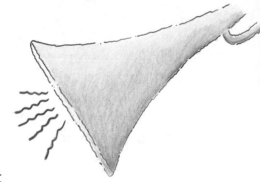

"Who is this 'author' person? I don't believe in any author," said someone else.

"There is no author. Each of us is his own author," said one of the new-agey types.

"It's a trick! Don't listen to the voice!" another yelled.

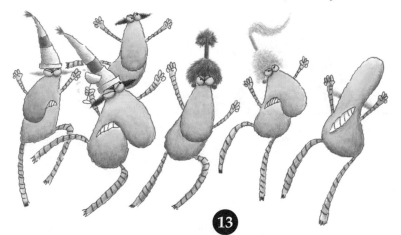

The characters were mad. "Let's tear down the loud speaker!" they said.

At that, the angry crowd ripped the page number from the bottom of the page and threw it up at the speaker.

The speaker came crashing to the ground.

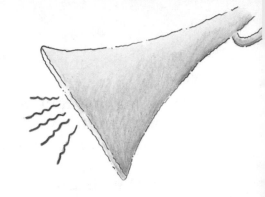

14

Well. This was very insulting to the author. Especially that bit where they threw the page number.

In no time, the characters were back to their yelling and party-ing, even forming a conga line around the edges of the page.

They were making a mess of *PageLand*.

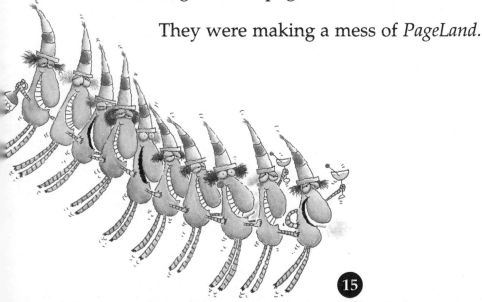

Although it would have been easy to end the story right here on page 16, the author didn't really want to do so. He *liked PageLand*. So he had one last idea.

"I will write in a *new* character," said the author. "Someone they can relate to and talk to because he will be like them."

So that is what the author did.

Here is the new character.

His name will be Arthur.

Arthur went to talk to the others.

"Excuse me," said Arthur. "Could I have your attention?"

Everyone gathered around the center of the page, eyeing the stranger.

"Who are you?" they asked. "We haven't seen you before."

"I know," he said. "My name is Arthur, and I have been sent here by the author. The author speaks through me, and there are three things he wants me to tell you."

"OK. Like what?" they asked, obviously just humoring him.

"Well," Arthur continued, "the first thing is, the author isn't very happy with the way you are acting. This story is supposed to be about love and sharing and working together. But so far, you guys are just making a big mess."

"What do you mean, 'this story'?" someone asked.

"That's the second thing I'm here to tell you. You are all characters in a book called *PageLand*." Arthur motioned with his hands to indicate the edges of the page. "See? You live on a page. You have been created by the author. It's time you realized that."

The characters gasped. Some tried to cover the ears of the children.

"If the author is writing us," said one character mockingly, "why doesn't he just write love and sharing and working together into the story himself? If we're just characters, the author is writing our words anyway. We can't make choices. We have no free will."

"Not true," said Arthur. "Haven't you ever written a story or painted a picture before? Even though you are creating it, it kind of takes on a life of its own and turns out in some surprising ways. The creator gives freedom to the creation. Likewise, even as the author writes our words, we bring some life to it. So you *do* have a choice."

Everyone fell silent. This was getting weird.

"And now, there's one final thing I have to tell you," Arthur continued. "As I said, you are all living in a book. And what do all books have in common?"

No one would answer.

Arthur answered his own question: "The thing all books have in common is that they all end. And this book will end too."

"Wh . . . when?" someone asked.

Arthur's voice was solemn. "I don't know. But it could end on the next page or many, many pages from now. But it will end. That is certain. The last page will turn, the back cover will close, and the story will be over."

"And what happens to us when the book ends?" someone asked, his voice shaking a little.

"Why, you stay behind,
trapped on the page,"
Arthur said calmly.

For a long moment it was silent except for one guy who had begun hyperventilating.

Finally, someone spoke.

"Well, this is just great," one said. "You come and interrupt our fun and get everyone all upset by saying we're in a book and it's going to end. So what do you expect us to do about it?"

Arthur replied, "I expect — and the author expects (we're the same person, actually) — that you change the course the story is taking. Make this into a story about love and sharing and working together. Come back to the author. That's all. Just change the story, and you won't have to worry about the end of the book. I'll take care of that."

The people were afraid.
And, as is often the case with fear,
it was turning into anger.

Just then, one of the children spoke.

"Excuse me, Mr. Arthur," the little one said, tugging at his pants leg. "I want to be part of a story that's about love and sharing and working together. But I don't know how."

Arthur smiled. "That's OK. Just stick with me," he said, stretching out his hand. "I'll show you."

At this point, the people's anger exploded.

"He's a liar!"
came another
voice.

"He's crazy!"
said another.

"No! Don't
listen to him!"
a man yelled
to the little one.

"Someone
stop him!"

Then, someone reached up into the text and grabbed a word. It was the word *liar*.

The man threw the word at Arthur.

liar

Then, someone threw another word. And then another. Soon, the entire crowd had joined in, assaulting Arthur with words.

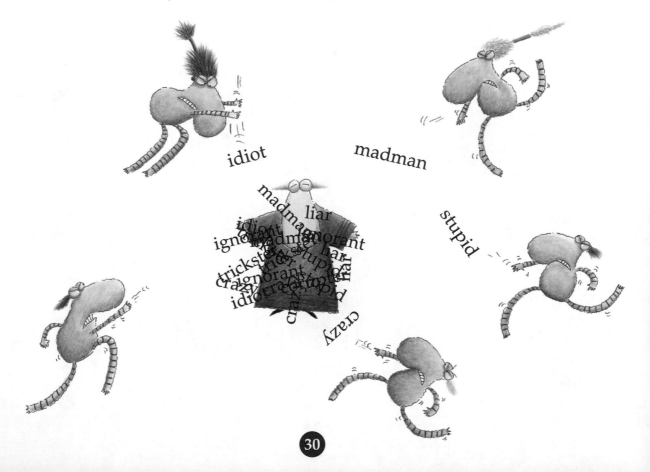

idiot

madman

stupid

madman liar idiot ignorant trickster liar crazy ignorant idiot stupid crazy

Within moments Arthur was buried beneath a heavy pile of words. At first he struggled under their weight. But his resistance became weaker and weaker.

They all stood there until Arthur stopped moving altogether. It was silent.

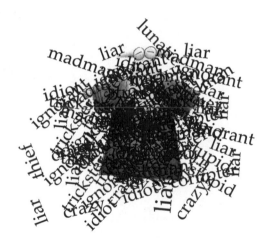

Everyone left.

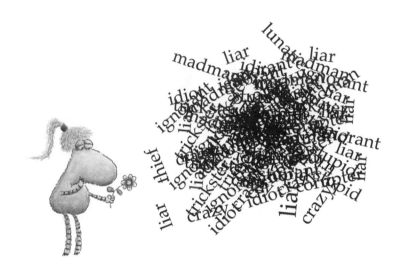

Arthur was gone, and the little one felt alone and afraid. She looked around. Maybe she could see this author whom Arthur had spoken about.

She called off the side of the page. "Hello? Are you there, author?"

Nothing.

She even tried to look straight ahead, past the page. "Yoohoo! Can you see me?" she cried. "Are you listening to me?

"Are you even real?"

But it was no use. She could not see the author.

Meanwhile, on page 36, the characters had gone back to their old ways. They were acting worse than ever.

The pages were becoming smudged. Random letters and punctuation were littered about on the ground.
Several people had even begun a game of soccer using the page numbers.

"Here's to the end of the story," they laughed.

"Yes, yes! The end of the story!"

"And when the last page comes, we'll just pick up a pencil and keep writing the story! We can live forever!"

37

It was getting very

dark now.

At this point, the author would like to halt the story to apologize to you, the reader, who began reading *PageLand* thinking that it would be about love and sharing and working together.

But maybe it's not too late yet. The author had one more idea, one more plot twist, that could perhaps save *PageLand* from being totally ruined.

Here's the plot twist.

The little one saw Arthur and ran to him.

"Arthur!" The little one cried. "But . . . but . . . I thought you were . . ."

Arthur smiled at her. "I was," he said, "but I came back. Remember, since I'm part of the author I am not limited to the same laws as the rest of the characters in the story. I can pop right over to any page in the book, anytime I want. I could be at the beginning and the end, the first page and the last, all at the same time."

This was hard for the little one to understand because she could only live from page to page, in order, one at a time.

Her confusion must have appeared quite silly to someone who could see as much as Arthur. But it didn't matter. He was back.

And she was happy.

Arthur knelt down and looked her in the eye. "Now I have a special job for you," he said.

"What?" Her heart leaped.

"Help me tell the story."

"But I'm not very good with words," she said.

"Don't worry about the words. This book is already full of words. Just *be* the story."

At first, the little one did not understand this.

But she quickly discovered that she knew just what to do.

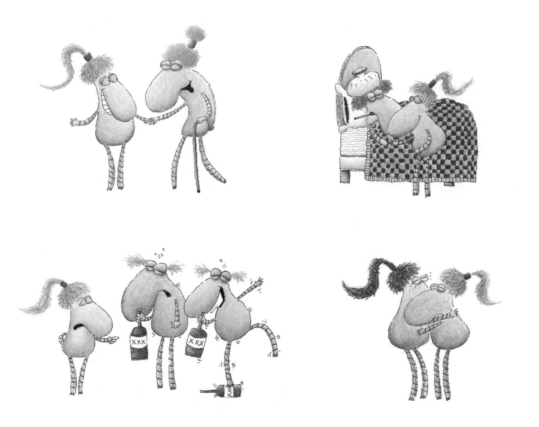

"Now, there's one more thing I have to tell you," Arthur told her. "And it might scare you. But don't let it because I'm going to stay with you, OK?"

"OK," the little one whispered. "What?"

"The end of the book
is just a few pages away," Arthur said.

The little one gasped.

"But . . . what about all the other characters?" she asked.

"They're back on page 38," Arthur said sadly. "And that's where most of them are going to stay. After the reader closes the back cover, they will be stuck in the darkness. That was their choice."

"And what about me and my new friends?" she asked, her voice trembling.

"You and your friends will be with the author. In fact, I'm taking *you* with me right now," Arthur said.

"Where?"

"It's hard to explain," Arthur said. "But have you ever read a story and liked one of the characters so much you always thought about them and it was like they became a part of you . . . long after you had forgotten the book? Well, it's kind of like that, but more real. The author will remember you, and you will be with him forever."

"I don't understand," she said. She was crying now, although she didn't know why.

"That's OK. There's only a few pages left. We don't have much time. Here . . . I want you to hold my hand and follow me to the top of the page.

"Keep your eyes focused on me. Don't look down."

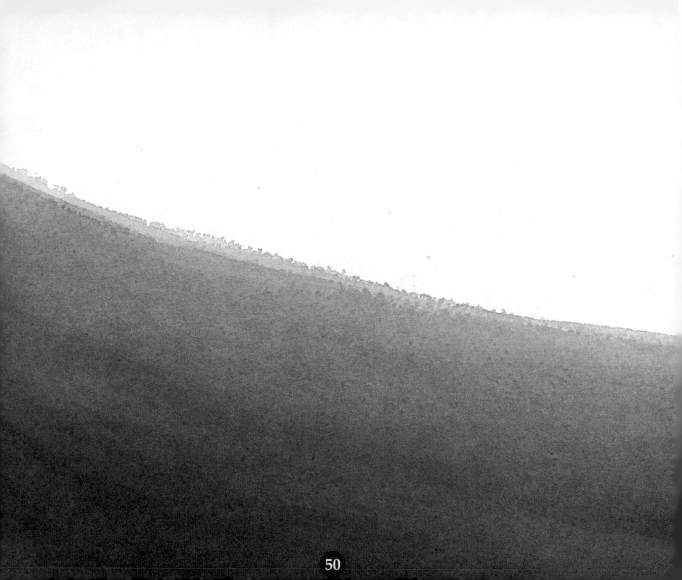

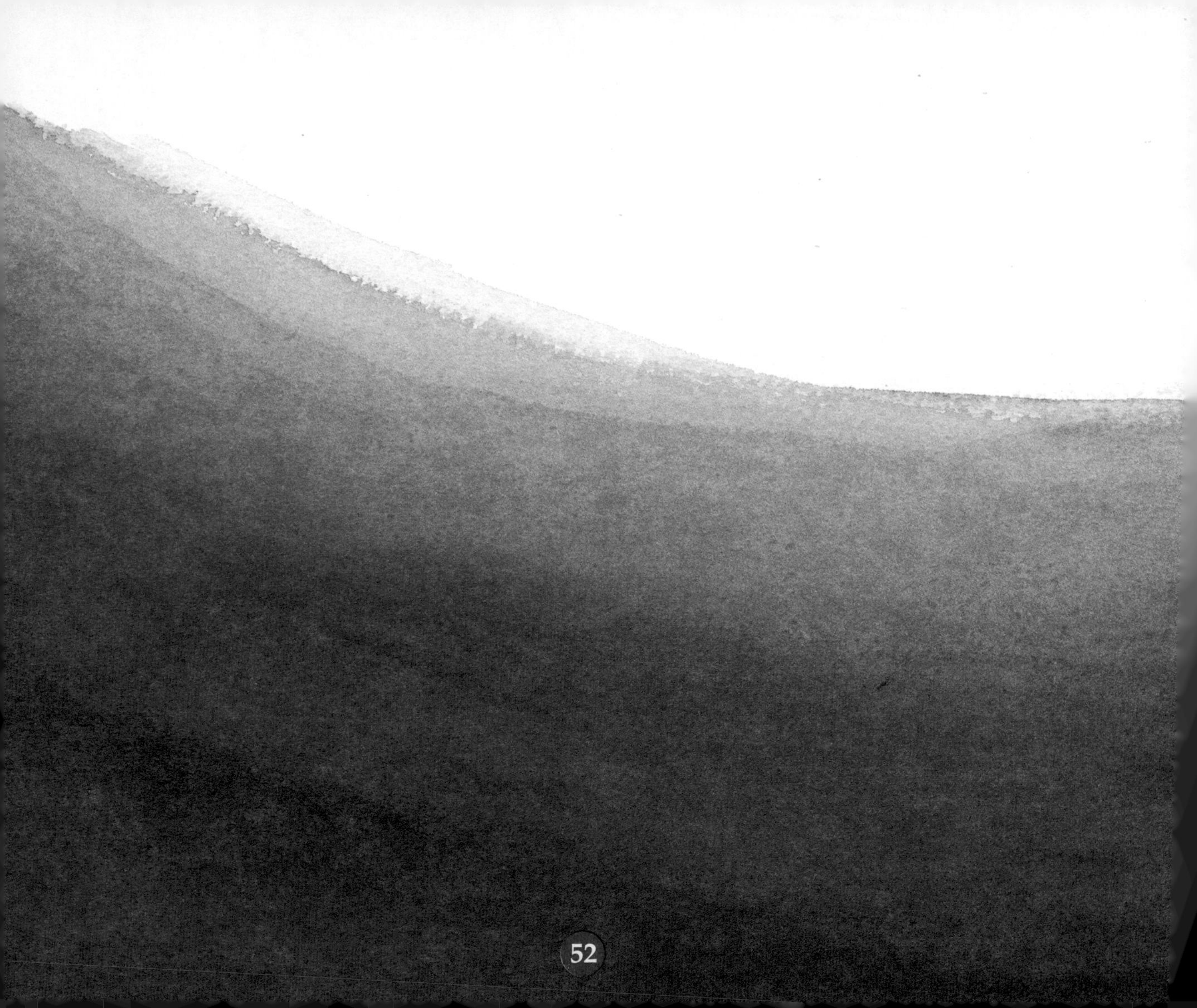

The end.

"Wait . . . don't close the back cover yet . . .
please . . . I'm begging you . . ."

"God utters me like a word containing a partial thought of Himself.
A word will never be able to comprehend the voice that utters it."
— *Thomas Merton*
Famous theologian and writer

"Let us fix our eyes on Jesus, the author and perfecter of our faith."
— *The apostle named Paul*
Hebrews 12:2